Estimate the sums by rounding the numbers and adding mentally. (Round to the place that makes sense for each number or problem.)

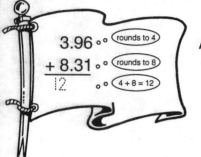

3.96 ∘∘ (rounds to 4)
$+ 8.31$ ∘∘ (rounds to 8)
12 ∘∘ (4 + 8 = 12)

A.
```
   2.04          6.014          10.33
 + 5.75        + 3.275        + 17.4
```

B.
```
  87.43          1.28          61.29          22.14
+ 80.40        + 9.40        + 59.24        + 95.52
```

C.
```
   5.37         29.34          70.16         256.11
 + 3.79       + 34.56        + 45.42        + 29.93
```

D.
```
  24.92         74.89          19.55         124.95
  76.38         27.36           4.46          59.50
+ 67.21       + 56.03        + 20.26       + 100.40
```

Rough Estimates

Estimate the differences by rounding the numbers and subtracting mentally.
(Round to the place that makes sense for each number or problem.)

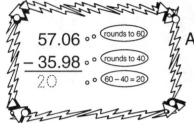

57.06 °° (rounds to 60)
− 35.98 °° (rounds to 40)
20 °° (60 − 40 = 20)

A.
```
    8  16
    9.67          5.03          11.20
  − 3.81        − 4.21         − 9.67
    5.86
```

B.
```
    12.40         19.05         32.79         12.89
  − 10.66        − 4.41       − 12.19        − 5.24
```

C.
```
    69.05         10.71         52.74         46.83
  − 19.55       − 10.69       − 13.14       − 20.91
```

D.
```
    55.70         68.30          8.13         32.78
  − 51.42       − 45.75        − 7.95       − 18.29
```

E.
```
    42.90         18.05          9.46         32.13
  − 19.72        − 8.68        − 1.78        − 1.97
```

Sum It Up

Find the sums.

A.
$$6.2 + 1.73 = 7.93$$
$$0.525 + 0.139$$
$$12.36 + 8.75$$
$$7.65 + 3.34$$

B.
$$72.88 + 14.75$$
$$9.89 + 42.69$$
$$0.25 + 0.73$$
$$5.9 + 6.057$$

C.
$$4.769 + 3.825$$
$$78.9 + 32.6$$
$$34.9 + 67.85$$
$$1.79 + 3.826$$

D.
$$4.7 + 8.8 + 0.45$$
$$439.6 + 7.049 + 12.32$$
$$72.6 + 123.12 + 2.4$$
$$2.36 + 3.78 + 2.67$$

E.
$$7.84 + 65.3 + 238.72$$
$$179.6 + 4.98 + 56.43$$
$$2.368 + 3.26 + 0.471$$

Decimal Differences

Find the differences.

A.
$$265.3 - 121.44 = 143.86$$

$$3.74 - 1.88$$

$$52.67 - 24.7$$

B.
$$5.25 - 3.87$$

$$0.85 - 0.68$$

$$51.04 - 22.63$$

$$70.00 - 16.95$$

C.
$$26.85 - 15.97$$

$$71.35 - 4.661$$

$$73.21 - 56.56$$

$$54.135 - 27.950$$

D.
$$23.9 - 18.72$$

$$44.04 - 28.15$$

$$1.343 - 0.975$$

$$680.3 - 136.9$$

E.
$$56.53 - 17.6$$

$$213.06 - 4.8$$

$$1.04 - 0.999$$

$$8.35 - 2.967$$

F.
$$439.3 - 97.42$$

$$83.81 - 7.96$$

$$100.1 - 83.79$$

$$17.31 - 14.9$$

Product Estimates

Estimate the products by rounding the numbers and multiplying. (Round to the place that makes sense for each number or problem.)

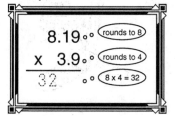

A.
$$32.9 \times 8.6$$
$$43.82 \times 17.9$$
$$8.97 \times 56.3$$

B.
$$52.7 \times 1.87$$
$$19.97 \times 4.95$$
$$3.7 \times 8.3$$
$$6.47 \times 7.19$$

C.
$$71.974 \times 8.6$$
$$67.46 \times 39.28$$
$$319.3 \times 86.76$$
$$909.36 \times 6.2$$

D.
$$9.15 \times 57.8$$
$$6.45 \times 8.59$$
$$7.83 \times 0.84$$
$$48.42 \times 2.26$$

E.
$$3.62 \times 7.8$$
$$26.9 \times 7.3$$
$$43.46 \times 37.3$$
$$808.2 \times 5.8$$

FS-11039 Pre-Algebra Activities

Multiplying Decimals

Find the products.

A.
     3.5
  x 6.7

     8.09
  x 5.7

     12.5
  x 0.74

     9.4
  x 2.7

B.
     5.12
  x 7.6

     9.12
  x 6.8

     0.73
  x 4.2

     5.6
  x 8.3

C.
     8.42
  x 7.3

     7.58
  x 4.8

     53.7
  x 6.9

     4.86
  x 3.7

Use estimation to see if your answers are reasonable.

D.
     7.25
  x 1.89

     5.62
  x 3.84

     3.79
  x 1.01

FS-11039 Pre-Algebra Activities

Quotient Estimates

Estimate the quotients by rounding the numbers and dividing. (Round to the place that makes sense for each number or problem.)

176.2 ÷ 6.3
That's close to 180 ÷ 6, so the quotient will be about 30.

A. 176.2 ÷ 63 = _____

B. 301.38 ÷ 5.3 = _____

C. 11.93 ÷ 3.2 = _____

D. 12.398 ÷ 4.1 = _____   162.58 ÷ 4.4 = _____

E. 482.04 ÷ 8.32 = _____   14.948 ÷ 5.1 = _____

F. 359.6 ÷ 8.5 = _____   266.7 ÷ 3.1 = _____

G. 64.26 ÷ 8.3 = _____   12.345 ÷ 3.3 = _____

H. 354.64 ÷ 69.3 = _____   1,615.9 ÷ 4.35 = _____

I. 413.66 ÷ 5.1 = _____   279.31 ÷ 4.1 = _____

J. 3,112.4 ÷ 5.2 = _____   363.63 ÷ 3.6 = _____

K. 409.4 ÷ 48.4 = _____   123.94 ÷ 3.9 = _____

L. 54.43 ÷ 9.32 = _____   34.594 ÷ 4.8 = _____

FS-11039 Pre-Algebra Activities

Decimal Division

Find the quotients.

A. $0.4\overline{)26}$ $0.5\overline{)29}$

B. $0.25\overline{)10}$ $3.4\overline{)12.92}$ $0.67\overline{)4.221}$

C. $9.5\overline{)0.8265}$ $0.7\overline{)22.4}$ $0.08\overline{)1.456}$

Super Shoppers

$0.67

$0.85

$1.20 PER LB.

SALAD BAR $2.50 PER LB.

TOMATO SAUCE

1 LB. SPAGHETTI

$1.59

Solve the problems. Circle your answers.

A. Sue bought 3 cans of tomato sauce. How much did she spend?	B. Sean spent $5.00 in all. He bought a package of rolls and some salad. How many pounds of salad did he buy?
C. Jorge bought a package of rolls and 2 pounds of salad. How much did he spend?	D. Patrick can buy a 5-pound box of spaghetti for $7.50. How much less expensive is this than buying five 1-pound boxes?
E. Emily spent $8.75 at the salad bar. How much salad did she buy?	F. How many pounds of mushrooms can Judy buy for $9.00?

Powers to the Numbers

Write in exponent form. Then find the value.
You may use a calculator to check your answers.

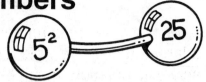

A. five squared   8 • 8 • 8 • 8   nine to the 4th power

_____   _____   _____

_____   _____   _____

B. 15 • 15 • 15   ten to the 5th power   seven cubed

_____   _____   _____

_____   _____   _____

C. one-half cubed   4 • 4 • 4 • 4 • 4   six to the 3rd power

_____   _____   _____

_____   _____   _____

D. 2.3 • 2.3 • 2.3   twelve squared   1.5 • 1.5 • 1.5 • 1.5

_____   _____   _____

_____   _____   _____

E. twenty cubed   7 • 7 • 7 • 7 • 7 • 7   one to the 12th power

_____   _____   _____

_____   _____   _____

Scientific Notation

Scientific notation is an easy way to represent a large number. To write a number in scientific notation, move the decimal point the number of places necessary to get a number from 1 to 9. Then write the number from 1 to 9 with a multiplication sign and a power of 10 showing the number of places you moved the decimal point.

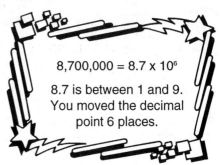

$8,700,000 = 8.7 \times 10^6$

8.7 is between 1 and 9. You moved the decimal point 6 places.

A. 5,300   70,000   260

   5.3×10^3 _____   _____

B. 450   8,200   45,300

   _____   _____   _____

C. 416,000   52,000   93,700

   _____   _____   _____

Write the numbers in standard form.

D. 3.5×10^2 4.37×10^4 9.7×10^5

   350   _____   _____

E. 3.4×10^3 8.37×10^5 1.05×10^2

   _____   _____   _____

Even Steven

A number is divisible by

2	3	4	5	6	9	10
if it ends in 0, 2, 4, 6, or 8	if the sum of the digits is divisible by 3	if the last two digits form a number that is divisible by 4	if it ends in 0 or 5	if it is divisible by 2 and 3	if the sum of the digits is divisible by 9	if it ends in 0

Complete the table. Write **Y** (yes) or **N** (no).

Number	Divisible by						
	2	3	4	5	6	9	10
540							
346							
621							
2,690							
5,211							
4,002							
6,732							
9,017							
10,950							
12,579							

Primo Primes

A prime number has only two whole-number factors—itself and 1.
A composite number has more than two whole-number factors.
Write **prime** or **composite** beside each number.

A.   3 _____

B.   18 _____

C.   64 _____

D.   10 _____

E.   6 _____

F.   5 _____

G.   49 _____

H.   53 _____

I.   89 _____

J.   43 _____

K.   73 _____

L.   67 _____

41 _____

19 _____

39 _____

11 _____

17 _____

51 _____

7 _____

85 _____

23 _____

79 _____

75 _____

83 _____

52 _____

15 _____

25 _____

36 _____

91 _____

13 _____

93 _____

47 _____

86 _____

29 _____

Perfect Products

List all of the factors of each number from least to greatest.
Then tell whether the number of factors is odd or even.

	Number	Factors	Odd or Even Number of Factors
A.	12	1, 2, 3, 4, 6, 12	Even
B.	16		
C.	18		
D.	20		
E.	25		
F.	32		
G.	36		
H.	40		
I.	48		
J.	56		
K.	60		
L.	64		
M.	72		
N.	81		
O.	100		
P.	121		

Look at the numbers that have an odd number of factors.
The middle factor of each number should be the square root of the number.

Find the Prime Factors

Draw a factor tree to find the prime factors. Then write the prime factors using exponents.

A.   75

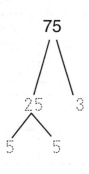

25   3

5   5

$5^2 \cdot 3$

_____

88

3^2 5^2

_____

B.   20

50

_____   _____

C.   98

90

_____   _____

15

Factors Are Great!

On scratch paper, find the factors for each number. Write the **greatest common factor** (GCF) for each pair of numbers on the line below the pair.

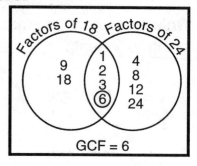

Factors of 18   Factors of 24

9
18

1
2
3
6

4
8
12
24

GCF = 6

A. 16 and 40   10 and 21

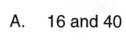

B. 24 and 40   36 and 54   48 and 64

C. 18 and 27   12 and 36   21 and 28

D. 16 and 24   18 and 30   8 and 27

E. 45 and 60   28 and 42   48 and 72

F. 26 and 51   100 and 130   24 and 72

G. 27 and 81   18 and 32   42 and 56

Multiples, at Least

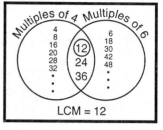

On scratch paper, find the multiples of each number. Write the **least common multiple** (LCM) for each pair of numbers on the line below the pair.

A. 5 and 9   4 and 18

_____   _____

B. 3 and 4   6 and 21   18 and 27

_____   _____   _____

C. 4 and 10   8 and 18   9 and 36

_____   _____   _____

D. 20 and 25   18 and 30   30 and 70

_____   _____   _____

Rewrite each pair of fractions using the LCM.

E. $\frac{2}{9}$ and $\frac{4}{15}$ $\frac{3}{4}$ and $\frac{1}{6}$ $\frac{2}{3}$ and $\frac{4}{5}$

_____   _____   _____

F. $\frac{3}{5}$ and $\frac{1}{2}$ $\frac{5}{8}$ and $\frac{3}{4}$ $\frac{2}{3}$ and $\frac{3}{4}$

_____   _____   _____

G. $\frac{3}{7}$ and $\frac{3}{5}$ $\frac{7}{9}$ and $\frac{5}{6}$ $\frac{5}{6}$ and $\frac{3}{8}$

_____   _____   _____

Order These

Write in order from least to greatest. Use scratch paper if necessary.

Sometimes I use a number line and sometimes I use the LCM.

A. $\frac{1}{5}, \frac{1}{3}, \frac{1}{4}$ $\qquad$ $\frac{4}{9}, \frac{1}{2}, \frac{2}{3}$

$\frac{1}{5}, \frac{1}{4}, \frac{1}{3}$

_____ _____

B. $\frac{5}{6}, \frac{6}{7}, \frac{3}{21}$ $\qquad$ $\frac{5}{8}, \frac{1}{2}, \frac{3}{4}$

_____ _____

C. $\frac{2}{5}, \frac{1}{2}, \frac{3}{10}$ $\frac{3}{5}, \frac{1}{2}, \frac{1}{4}$ $\frac{3}{8}, \frac{2}{3}, \frac{1}{4}$

_____ _____ _____

D. $\frac{3}{4}, \frac{3}{5}, \frac{7}{10}$ $\frac{1}{3}, \frac{3}{8}, \frac{1}{4}$ $\frac{2}{5}, \frac{4}{9}, \frac{11}{15}$

_____ _____ _____

E. $\frac{2}{5}, \frac{1}{3}, \frac{1}{4}$ $\frac{2}{9}, \frac{5}{18}, \frac{3}{6}$ $\frac{5}{6}, \frac{4}{5}, \frac{3}{4}$

_____ _____ _____

F. $\frac{2}{3}, \frac{5}{6}, \frac{3}{4}$ $\frac{1}{2}, \frac{3}{10}, \frac{4}{9}$ $\frac{5}{6}, \frac{2}{5}, \frac{2}{3}$

_____ _____ _____

Watch the Signs

Add or subtract. Write your answer in the simplest form.

A.

$$\frac{2}{3}$$
$$+\ \frac{1}{3}$$

$$\frac{3}{3} = 1$$

$$\frac{1}{8}$$
$$+\ \frac{4}{8}$$

$$\frac{6}{11}$$
$$+\ \frac{2}{11}$$

$$\frac{10}{13}$$
$$-\ \frac{4}{13}$$

B.

$$\frac{11}{12}$$
$$-\ \frac{5}{12}$$

$$\frac{4}{9}$$
$$+\ \frac{2}{9}$$

$$\frac{2}{15}$$
$$+\ \frac{8}{15}$$

$$\frac{3}{20}$$
$$+\ \frac{11}{20}$$

C.

$$\frac{2}{5}$$
$$+\ \frac{1}{2}$$

$$\frac{7}{12}$$
$$+\ \frac{1}{4}$$

$$\frac{9}{10}$$
$$-\ \frac{1}{2}$$

$$\frac{2}{3}$$
$$-\ \frac{1}{6}$$

D.

$$\frac{13}{18}$$
$$-\ \frac{2}{9}$$

$$\frac{7}{24}$$
$$+\ \frac{5}{12}$$

$$\frac{5}{8}$$
$$-\ \frac{4}{7}$$

$$\frac{14}{15}$$
$$+\ \frac{8}{9}$$

E.

$$\frac{4}{9}$$
$$+\ \frac{3}{4}$$

$$\frac{2}{5}$$
$$+\ \frac{4}{15}$$

$$\frac{1}{3}$$
$$-\ \frac{1}{7}$$

19

FS-11039 Pre-Algebra Activities

Mixed Number Sums

Add. Write your answer in the simplest form.

I have to find the least common denominator first!

A.

$3\frac{1}{2}$
$+\ 2\frac{1}{6}$

$7\frac{3}{10}$
$+\ 9\frac{3}{4}$

B.

$12\frac{5}{6}$
$+\ \ 6\frac{7}{9}$

$6\frac{4}{7}$
$+\ 2\frac{9}{14}$

$8\frac{7}{12}$
$+\ 6\frac{5}{8}$

$11\frac{1}{6}$
$+\ \ 7\frac{1}{2}$

C.

$1\frac{5}{6}$
$+\ 6\frac{1}{2}$

$7\frac{2}{3}$
$+\ 6\frac{3}{5}$

$4\frac{1}{4}$
$+\ 7\frac{7}{8}$

$3\frac{2}{3}$
$+\ 2\frac{2}{3}$

D.

$6\frac{1}{6}$
$+\ 1\frac{11}{12}$

$3\frac{3}{4}$
$+\ 6\frac{1}{2}$

$2\frac{5}{6}$
$+\ 5\frac{3}{4}$

$2\frac{1}{8}$
$+\ 8\frac{2}{3}$

E.

$3\frac{1}{3}$
$4\frac{5}{6}$
$+\ 1\frac{1}{12}$

$6\frac{2}{3}$
$1\frac{1}{3}$
$+\ 3\frac{1}{2}$

$5\frac{1}{2}$
$2\frac{1}{3}$
$+\ 11\frac{1}{6}$

$2\frac{1}{2}$
$1\frac{5}{8}$
$+\ 3\frac{3}{4}$

FS-11039 Pre-Algebra Activities

Mixed Number Differences

Subtract. Write your answer in the simplest form.

A.

$$8\frac{4}{5}$$
$$-\ 4\frac{1}{2}$$

$$7\frac{3}{10}$$
$$-\ 6\frac{3}{4}$$

$$9\frac{7}{9}$$
$$-\ 5\frac{1}{3}$$

$$8\frac{3}{4}$$
$$-\ 2\frac{5}{8}$$

B.

$$6\frac{5}{6}$$
$$-\ 3\frac{7}{9}$$

$$2\frac{1}{9}$$
$$-\ \ \ \frac{1}{2}$$

$$18\frac{1}{3}$$
$$-\ \ 9$$

$$17\frac{3}{5}$$
$$-\ \ 6\frac{1}{3}$$

C.

$$4\frac{9}{10}$$
$$-\ 3\frac{2}{5}$$

$$4\frac{5}{8}$$
$$-\ 1\frac{1}{4}$$

$$4\frac{7}{9}$$
$$-\ 2\frac{4}{9}$$

$$3\frac{3}{10}$$
$$-\ 2$$

D.

$$5\frac{9}{10}$$
$$-\ 4\frac{3}{5}$$

$$3$$
$$-\ 1\frac{7}{10}$$

$$6\frac{3}{8}$$
$$-\ 2\frac{3}{16}$$

$$4\frac{1}{10}$$
$$-\ 2\frac{3}{10}$$

E.

$$8\frac{1}{4}$$
$$-\ 4\frac{3}{4}$$

$$12\frac{2}{5}$$
$$-\ \ 8\frac{9}{10}$$

$$15\frac{1}{2}$$
$$-\ \ 9\frac{9}{16}$$

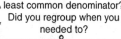

Did you remember to find the least common denominator? Did you regroup when you needed to?

Fraction Practice

Add or subtract. Write your answers in the simplest form.

A. $\dfrac{1}{5}$ $\dfrac{3}{4}$

$+\dfrac{3}{10}$ $-\dfrac{3}{8}$

B. $\dfrac{4}{5}$ $9\dfrac{1}{8}$ $16\dfrac{5}{11}$ $6\dfrac{4}{7}$

$+1\dfrac{5}{6}$ $+6\dfrac{3}{4}$ $-\ 9$ $+2\dfrac{1}{5}$

C. $13\dfrac{1}{3}$ 7 $8\dfrac{1}{12}$ $5\dfrac{9}{14}$

$+\ 9\dfrac{8}{17}$ $-6\dfrac{1}{8}$ $+3\dfrac{1}{3}$ $-3\dfrac{6}{7}$

D. 6 $6\dfrac{7}{11}$ $4\dfrac{1}{2}$ $9\dfrac{3}{7}$

$-1\dfrac{19}{21}$ $+3$ $+10\dfrac{11}{14}$ $-4\dfrac{1}{6}$

E. $\dfrac{5}{12}$ $15\dfrac{1}{7}$ $5\dfrac{9}{10}$ $9\dfrac{1}{4}$

$+4\dfrac{5}{6}$ $-6\dfrac{2}{3}$ $+1\dfrac{1}{2}$ $-3\dfrac{2}{5}$

Products From Fractions

Multiply. Divide any numerator and denominator by a common factor to make the fractions easier to multiply. Write your answers in the simplest form.

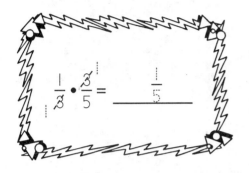

$$\frac{1}{3} \cdot \frac{3}{5} = \underline{\hspace{2cm}} \quad \frac{1}{5}$$

A. $\frac{1}{4} \cdot \frac{4}{9} = \underline{\hspace{3cm}}$

B. $\frac{7}{8} \cdot \frac{8}{7} = \underline{\hspace{3cm}}$

C. $\frac{7}{11} \cdot \frac{23}{42} = \underline{\hspace{3cm}}$

$\frac{3}{8} \cdot \frac{4}{5} = \underline{\hspace{3cm}}$

D. $\frac{3}{2} \cdot \frac{5}{6} = \underline{\hspace{3cm}}$

$\frac{3}{4} \cdot \frac{2}{9} = \underline{\hspace{3cm}}$

E. $\frac{5}{7} \cdot \frac{7}{10} = \underline{\hspace{3cm}}$

$\frac{4}{5} \cdot \frac{1}{8} = \underline{\hspace{3cm}}$

F. $\frac{4}{7} \cdot \frac{7}{2} = \underline{\hspace{3cm}}$

$\frac{3}{5} \cdot \frac{25}{6} = \underline{\hspace{3cm}}$

G. $\frac{7}{8} \cdot \frac{4}{21} = \underline{\hspace{3cm}}$

$\frac{2}{11} \cdot \frac{11}{24} = \underline{\hspace{3cm}}$

H. $\frac{3}{5} \cdot \frac{2}{3} = \underline{\hspace{3cm}}$

$\frac{6}{7} \cdot \frac{5}{12} = \underline{\hspace{3cm}}$

I. $\frac{7}{10} \cdot \frac{5}{8} = \underline{\hspace{3cm}}$

$\frac{2}{7} \cdot \frac{7}{8} = \underline{\hspace{3cm}}$

Mixed Number Multiplication

Find the products. Rewrite mixed numbers as improper fractions before you multiply. Write your answers in the simplest form.

A. $\dfrac{\cancel{16}^{4}}{1} \cdot \dfrac{3}{\cancel{4}_{1}} =$ _____ $\dfrac{12}{1} = 12$

B. $6\dfrac{2}{3} \cdot \dfrac{1}{4} =$ _____ $5\dfrac{1}{8} \cdot 6 =$ _____

C. $7\dfrac{1}{7} \cdot \dfrac{3}{8} =$ _____ $7\dfrac{3}{4} \cdot 20 =$ _____

D. $1\dfrac{1}{3} \cdot 30 =$ _____ $2\dfrac{1}{2} \cdot \dfrac{5}{6} =$ _____

E. $\dfrac{3}{8} \cdot 7\dfrac{2}{3} =$ _____ $5\dfrac{1}{4} \cdot 16 =$ _____

F. $2\dfrac{2}{3} \cdot 4\dfrac{1}{2} =$ _____ $9\dfrac{7}{8} \cdot 2\dfrac{2}{3} =$ _____

G. $4\dfrac{2}{11} \cdot 22 =$ _____ $18 \cdot 7\dfrac{4}{9} =$ _____

H. $4\dfrac{2}{5} \cdot 25 =$ _____ $5\dfrac{1}{3} \cdot 9\dfrac{1}{8} =$ _____

I. $15 \cdot 9\dfrac{2}{3} =$ _____ $2\dfrac{1}{4} \cdot 11\dfrac{1}{3} =$ _____

How Many Equal Parts?

To divide fractions, rewrite the problem and multiply by the reciprocal of the divisor. Circle each quotient in the simplest form.

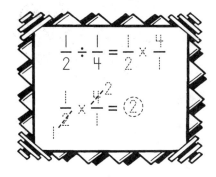

A. $\dfrac{8}{9} \div \dfrac{4}{5} =$ _____

B. $\dfrac{1}{2} \div \dfrac{3}{4} =$ _____

C. $\dfrac{3}{4} \div \dfrac{1}{2} =$ _____ $\dfrac{2}{3} \div \dfrac{1}{3} =$ _____

D. $\dfrac{4}{5} \div \dfrac{1}{8} =$ _____ $\dfrac{1}{3} \div \dfrac{1}{12} =$ _____

E. $\dfrac{4}{5} \div \dfrac{7}{5} =$ _____ $\dfrac{3}{4} \div \dfrac{1}{8} =$ _____

F. $\dfrac{1}{3} \div \dfrac{1}{2} =$ _____ $\dfrac{1}{3} \div \dfrac{1}{9} =$ _____

G. $\dfrac{5}{8} \div \dfrac{3}{4} =$ _____ $\dfrac{7}{10} \div \dfrac{2}{3} =$ _____

H. $\dfrac{5}{6} \div \dfrac{2}{3} =$ _____ $\dfrac{3}{10} \div \dfrac{1}{5} =$ _____

I. $\dfrac{5}{8} \div \dfrac{1}{4} =$ _____ $\dfrac{7}{2} \div \dfrac{3}{4} =$ _____

     FS-11039 Pre-Algebra Activities

Mixed Number Division

Change the mixed numbers to improper fractions. Then multiply the first fraction by the reciprocal of the second fraction. Circle each answer in the simplest form.

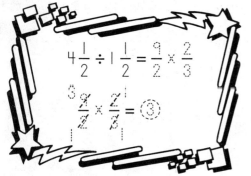

A. $4\frac{2}{3} \div 2 =$ _____

B. $6\frac{1}{4} \div 12\frac{1}{2} =$ _____

C. $7\frac{5}{6} \div 1\frac{5}{6} =$ _____

$5\frac{1}{4} \div 1\frac{1}{6} =$ _____

D. $15 \div 1\frac{1}{2} =$ _____

$6\frac{1}{4} \div 5 =$ _____

E. $\frac{2}{3} \div 1\frac{1}{3} =$ _____

$18 \div 7\frac{1}{5} =$ _____

F. $1\frac{1}{2} \div \frac{3}{8} =$ _____

$2\frac{4}{7} \div 2 =$ _____

G. $1\frac{1}{2} \div 4\frac{1}{2} =$ _____

$3\frac{1}{4} \div 1\frac{3}{8} =$ _____

H. $2\frac{1}{2} \div 1\frac{1}{2} =$ _____

$10 \div 3\frac{1}{3} =$ _____

I. $2\frac{4}{5} \div 6\frac{2}{3} =$ _____

$2\frac{2}{3} \div 1\frac{1}{6} =$ _____

Pull-Out Answers

Page 1
Estimates will vary. Possible estimates are given.
A. 8; 9; 27
B. 170; 10; 120; 120
C. 9; 60; 120; 290
D. 170; 160; 44; 280

Page 2
Estimates will vary. Possible estimates are given.
A. 6; 1; 1
B. 1; 16; 21; 8
C. 50; 0; 40; 30
D. 5; 20; 0; 10
E. 20; 9; 7; 28

Page 3
A. 7.93; 0.664; 21.11; 10.99
B. 87.63; 52.58; 0.98; 11.957
C. 8.594; 111.5; 102.75; 5.616
D. 13.95; 458.969; 198.12; 8.81
E. 311.86; 241.01; 6.099

Page 4
A. 143.86; 1.86; 27.97
B. 1.38; 0.17; 28.41; 53.05
C. 10.88; 66.689; 16.65; 26.185
D. 5.18; 15.89; 0.368; 543.4
E. 38.93; 208.26; 0.041; 5.383
F. 341.88; 75.85; 16.31; 2.41

Page 5
Estimates will vary. Possible estimates are given.
A. 270; 800; 540
B. 100; 100; 32; 42
C. 630; 2,800; 27,000; 5,400
D. 540; 54; 7; 100
E. 32; 210; 1,600; 4,800

Page 6
A. 23.45; 46.113; 9.25; 25.38
B. 38.912; 62.016; 3.066; 46.48
C. 61.466; 36.384; 370.53; 17.982
D. 13.7025; 21.5808; 3.8279

Page 7
Estimates will vary. Possible estimates are given.
A. 3   G. 8; 4
B. 60   H. 5; 400
C. 4   I. 80; 70
D. 3; 40   J. 600; 100
E. 60; 3   K. 8; 30
F. 40; 90   L. 6; 7

Page 8
A. 65; 58
B. 40; 3.8; 6.3
C. 0.087; 32; 18.2

Page 9
A. $2.01
B. 1.66 pounds
C. $5.85
D. $0.45 less expensive
E. 3.5 pounds
F. 7.5 pounds

Page 10
A. 5^2 25; 8^4 4,096; 9^4 6,561
B. 15^3 3,375; 10^5 100,000; 7^3 343
C. $(\frac{1}{2})^3$ $\frac{1}{8}$; 4^5 1,024; 6^3 216
D. $(2.3)^3$ 12.167; 12^2 144; $(1.5)^4$ 5.0625
E. 20^3 8,000; 7^6 117,649; 1^{12} 1

Page 11
A. 5.3×10^3; 7×10^4; 2.6×10^2
B. 4.5×10^2; 8.2×10^3; 4.53×10^4
C. 4.16×10^5; 5.2×10^4; 9.37×10^4
D. 350; 43,700; 970,000
E. 3,400; 837,000; 105

Page 12

A number is divisible by

2	3	4	5	6	9	10
if it ends in 0, 2, 4, 6, or 8	if the sum of the digits is divisible by 3	if the last two digits form a number that is divisible by 4	if it ends in 0 or 5	if it is divisible by 2 and 3	if the sum of the digits is divisible by 9	if it ends in 0

Complete the table. Write Y (yes) or N (no).

Number	Divisible by						
	2	3	4	5	6	9	10
540	Y	Y	Y	Y	Y	Y	Y
346	Y	N	N	N	N	N	N
621	N	Y	N	N	N	Y	N
2,690	Y	N	N	Y	N	N	Y
5,211	N	Y	N	N	N	Y	N
4,002	Y	Y	N	N	Y	N	N
6,732	Y	Y	Y	N	Y	Y	N
9,017	N	N	N	N	N	N	N
10,950	Y	Y	N	Y	Y	N	Y
12,579	N	Y	N	N	N	N	N

Page 13
A. prime; prime
B. composite; prime
C. composite; composite; composite
D. composite; prime; composite
E. composite; prime; composite
F. prime; composite; composite
G. composite; prime; composite
H. prime; composite; prime
I. prime; prime; composite
J. prime; prime; prime
K. prime; composite; composite
L. prime; prime; prime

Pull-Out Answers

Page 14
A. 1, 2, 3, 4, 6, 12; even
B. 1, 2, 4, 8, 16; odd
C. 1, 2, 3, 6, 9, 18; even
D. 1, 2, 4, 5, 10, 20; even
E. 1, 5, 25; odd
F. 1, 2, 4, 8, 16, 32; even
G. 1, 2, 3, 4, 6, 9, 12, 18, 36; odd
H. 1, 2, 4, 5, 8, 10, 20, 40; even
I. 1, 2, 3, 4, 6, 8, 12, 16, 24, 48; even
J. 1, 2, 4, 7, 8, 14, 28, 56; even
K. 1, 2, 3, 4, 5, 6, 10, 12, 15, 20, 30, 60; even
L. 1, 2, 4, 8, 16, 32, 64; odd
M. 1, 2, 3, 4, 6, 8, 9, 12, 18, 24, 36, 72; even
N. 1, 3, 9, 27, 81; odd
O. 1, 2, 4, 5, 10, 20, 25, 50, 100; odd
P. 1, 11, 121; odd

Page 15
A. $5^2 \cdot 3$; $2^3 \cdot 11$
B. $2^2 \cdot 5$; $5^2 \cdot 2$
C. $7^2 \cdot 2$; $3^2 \cdot 5 \cdot 2$

Page 16
A. 8; 1
B. 8; 18; 16
C. 9; 12; 7
D. 8; 6; 1
E. 15; 14; 24
F. 1; 10; 24
G. 27; 2; 14

Page 17
A. 45; 36
B. 12; 42; 54
C. 20; 72; 36
D. 100; 90; 210
E. $\frac{10}{45}$ and $\frac{12}{45}$
   $\frac{9}{12}$ and $\frac{2}{12}$
   $\frac{10}{15}$ and $\frac{12}{15}$
F. $\frac{6}{10}$ and $\frac{5}{10}$
   $\frac{5}{8}$ and $\frac{6}{8}$
   $\frac{9}{12}$ and $\frac{9}{12}$
G. $\frac{15}{35}$ and $\frac{21}{35}$
   $\frac{14}{18}$ and $\frac{15}{18}$
   $\frac{20}{24}$ and $\frac{9}{24}$

Page 18
A. $\frac{1}{5}$, $\frac{1}{4}$, $\frac{1}{3}$; $\frac{4}{9}$, $\frac{1}{2}$, $\frac{2}{3}$
B. $\frac{3}{8}$, $\frac{5}{6}$, $\frac{6}{7}$; $\frac{1}{2}$, $\frac{5}{8}$, $\frac{3}{4}$
C. $\frac{3}{10}$, $\frac{2}{5}$, $\frac{1}{2}$; $\frac{1}{4}$, $\frac{1}{2}$, $\frac{3}{5}$; $\frac{1}{4}$, $\frac{3}{8}$, $\frac{2}{3}$
D. $\frac{3}{5}$, $\frac{7}{10}$, $\frac{3}{4}$; $\frac{1}{4}$, $\frac{1}{3}$, $\frac{3}{8}$; $\frac{2}{3}$, $\frac{4}{9}$, $\frac{11}{15}$
E. $\frac{1}{4}$, $\frac{1}{3}$, $\frac{2}{5}$; $\frac{2}{9}$, $\frac{5}{18}$, $\frac{3}{6}$; $\frac{3}{4}$, $\frac{4}{5}$, $\frac{5}{6}$
F. $\frac{2}{3}$, $\frac{3}{4}$, $\frac{5}{6}$; $\frac{3}{10}$, $\frac{4}{9}$, $\frac{1}{2}$; $\frac{2}{5}$, $\frac{2}{3}$, $\frac{5}{6}$

Page 19
A. 1; $\frac{5}{8}$; $\frac{8}{11}$; $\frac{6}{13}$
B. $\frac{1}{2}$; $\frac{2}{5}$; $\frac{2}{3}$; $\frac{7}{10}$
C. $\frac{9}{10}$; $\frac{5}{6}$; $\frac{2}{5}$; $\frac{1}{2}$
D. $\frac{1}{2}$; $\frac{17}{24}$; $\frac{5}{56}$; $1\frac{37}{45}$
E. $1\frac{7}{36}$; $\frac{2}{3}$; $\frac{4}{21}$

Page 20
A. $5\frac{2}{3}$; $17\frac{1}{20}$
B. $19\frac{11}{18}$; $9\frac{3}{14}$; $15\frac{5}{24}$; $18\frac{2}{3}$
C. $8\frac{1}{3}$; $14\frac{4}{15}$; $12\frac{1}{8}$; $6\frac{1}{3}$
D. $8\frac{1}{12}$; $10\frac{1}{4}$; $8\frac{7}{12}$; $10\frac{19}{24}$
E. $9\frac{1}{4}$; $11\frac{1}{2}$; 19; $7\frac{7}{8}$

Page 21
A. $4\frac{3}{10}$; $\frac{11}{20}$; $4\frac{4}{5}$; $6\frac{1}{8}$
B. $3\frac{1}{18}$; $1\frac{11}{18}$; $9\frac{1}{2}$; $11\frac{1}{5}$
C. $1\frac{1}{2}$; $3\frac{3}{8}$; $2\frac{1}{3}$; $1\frac{3}{10}$
D. $1\frac{3}{10}$; $1\frac{3}{10}$; $4\frac{3}{16}$; $1\frac{4}{5}$
E. $3\frac{1}{2}$; $3\frac{1}{2}$; $5\frac{15}{16}$

Page 22
A. $\frac{1}{2}$; $\frac{3}{8}$
B. $2\frac{19}{30}$; $15\frac{7}{8}$; $7\frac{5}{11}$; $8\frac{27}{35}$
C. $22\frac{41}{51}$; $\frac{7}{8}$; $11\frac{5}{12}$; $1\frac{11}{14}$
D. $4\frac{2}{21}$; $9\frac{7}{11}$; $15\frac{5}{7}$; $5\frac{11}{42}$
E. $5\frac{1}{4}$; $8\frac{10}{21}$; $7\frac{5}{8}$; $5\frac{17}{20}$

Page 23
A. $\frac{1}{9}$
B. 1
C. $\frac{23}{66}$; $\frac{3}{10}$
D. $1\frac{1}{4}$; $\frac{1}{6}$
E. $\frac{1}{2}$; $\frac{1}{10}$
F. 2; $2\frac{1}{2}$
G. $\frac{1}{6}$; $\frac{1}{12}$
H. $\frac{2}{5}$; $\frac{5}{14}$
I. $\frac{7}{16}$; $\frac{1}{4}$

Page 24
A. 12
B. $1\frac{2}{3}$; $30\frac{3}{4}$
C. $2\frac{19}{28}$; 155
D. 40; $2\frac{1}{12}$
E. $2\frac{7}{8}$; 84
F. 12; $26\frac{1}{3}$
G. 92; 134
H. 110; $48\frac{2}{3}$
I. 145; $25\frac{1}{2}$

Page 25
A. $1\frac{1}{8}$
B. $\frac{2}{3}$
C. $1\frac{1}{2}$; 2
D. $6\frac{2}{3}$; 4
E. $\frac{4}{7}$; 6
F. $\frac{2}{3}$; 3
G. $\frac{5}{6}$; $1\frac{1}{20}$
H. $1\frac{1}{4}$; $1\frac{1}{2}$
I. $2\frac{1}{2}$; $4\frac{2}{3}$

Pull-Out Answers

Page 26

A. 2⅓
B. ½
C. 4³⁄₁₁; 4½
D. 10; 1¼
E. ½; 2½
F. 4; 1²⁄₇
G. ⅓; 2⁴⁄₁₁
H. 1⅔; 3
I. ²¹⁄₅₀; 2²⁄₇

Page 27

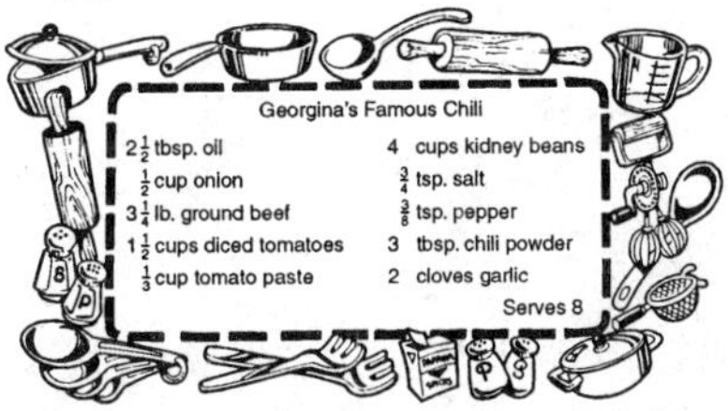

Revise the amount of each ingredient to serve the number of people shown.

Ingredient	16 servings	4 servings	20 servings	6 servings
oil	5 tbsp	1¼ tbsp	6¼ tbsp	1⅞ tbsp
onion	1 cup	¼ cup	1¼ cups	⅜ cup
ground beef	6½ lb.	1⅝ lb.	8⅛ lb.	2⁷⁄₁₆ lb.
tomatoes	3 cups	¾ cup	3¾ cups	1⅛ cups
tomato paste	⅔ cup	⅙ cup	⅚ cup	¼ cup
kidney beans	8 cups	2 cups	10 cups	3 cups
salt	1½ tsp.	⅜ tsp.	1⅞ tsp.	⁹⁄₁₆ tsp.
pepper	¾ tsp.	³⁄₁₆ tsp.	¹⁵⁄₁₆ tsp.	⁹⁄₃₂ tsp.
chili powder	6 tbsp.	1½ tbsp.	7½ tbsp.	2¼ tbsp.
garlic	4 cloves	1 clove	5 cloves	1 ½ cloves

Page 28

Vowel	Freq.	Cum. Freq.
a	8	8
e	16	24
i	7	31
o	12	43
u	3	46

A. 46
B. 9 more times
C. 24 times
D. less often

Page 29

A. 57 inches
B. 15 inches
C. 7 students
D. 3 students
E. 53 in., 54 in., 62 in., 65 in.
F. 20 students

Page 30

Stem	Leaves
5	6, 9
6	3, 5, 7, 8
7	4, 4, 6, 6, 8, 9
8	0, 2, 2, 3, 6, 7, 8, 8, 9
9	0, 0, 2, 2, 5, 5, 5

A. 56
B. 95
C. 7
D. 6
E. 15
F. 95

Page 31

Pictographs and answers will vary.

Page 32

Bar graphs will vary.
A. 4-door sedan and station wagon
B. 2-door sports
C. 300 more
D. compact cars and vans

Page 33

Line graphs will vary.
A. Saturday; Tuesday
B. Monday and Wednesday

Page 34

A. a range of weight
D. the number of players in the weight categories
C. 9 players
D. 121–135 pounds
E. 7 players

Page 35

Ms. Rowe—28; 84.4; 83; 79
Mrs. Midgely—21; 88.5; 86; 86
Mr. Maynard—32; 78.8; 73; 72
Mr. Arnaiz—26; 77.7; 78; 78
Ms. Silver—20; 76.9; 75; 75
Ms. Choi–26; 88.1; 89; 94

Page 36

A. 0
B. 13
C. 28
D. 41
E. 100

Page 37

A. 3
B. 1½; ⁴⁄₇
C. 2⅗; ⅓
D. ⁵⁄₁₇; ⁴⁄₉
E. 1½; ⅕
F. ⅛; 4
G. 1⅐; ⅓
H. ⅖; ½
I. ⅚; ⁴⁄₉
J. ⁵⁄₇; ⁵⁄₉
K. ⅔; ³⁄₂₀

Page 38

A. 8 in 1; 50 in 1
B. 5 in 1; 250 in 1
C. 6 in 1; 25 in 1
D. 12 in 1; 24 in 1
E. 55 in 1; 180 in 1
F. 86 in 1; 50 in 1
G. 40 in 1; 38 in 1

Page 39

A. yes; no; no
B. yes; no; yes
C. no; yes; yes
D. no; yes; yes
E. yes; no; yes
F. yes; yes; yes
G. no; no; no
H. no; yes; yes
I. yes; no; no
J. yes; yes

Pull-Out Answers

Page 40
A. 32; 10
B. 11; 2; 24; 4
C. 9; 5; 4; 2.1
D. 3; 18; 45; 3.75
E. 3; 35; 0.7; 39

Page 41
A. $0.32; $0.23
B. $0.06; $0.44; $0.31
C. $3.99; $0.24; $2.30
D. $1.11; $1.25; $0.97
E. $76.00; $2.25; $0.59
F. $0.44; $1.25; $13.40
G. $3.75; $0.11; $0.55
H. $1.58; $0.75; $2.78

Page 42
A. $0.25, $0.23
B. $0.21, $0.18
C. $0.60, $0.66
D. $1.99, $1.85
E. $1.10, $1.07
F. $0.18, $0.23
G. $2.29, $2.53
H. $0.06, $0.13

Page 43
A. 14; 16; 28.5
B. 2.25; 13.5; 38.5

Page 44
A. 35%; 17%
B. 41%; 45%
C. 23%; 75%; 72%
D. 81%; 1%; 25%
E. 27%; 50%; 43%
F. 31%; 10%; 40%
G. 5%; 39%; 60%
H. 9%; 80%; 8%
I. 63%; 20%; 45%
J. 71%; 86%; 23%
K. 97%; 7%; 70%

Page 45
A. 0.95; 0.82; 0.43
B. 0.17; 0.68; 0.48

C. 0.71; 0.04; 0.73
D. 0.55; 0.3; 0.1
E. 0.07; 0.15; 0.09
F. 0.84; 0.52; 0.32
G. 0.94; 0.02; 0.11
H. 0.5; 0.34; 0.05
I. 0.19; 1; 0.26
J. 0.2; 0.01; 0.16
K. 0.12; 0.21; 0.51
L. 0.06; 0.18; 0.03

Page 46
A. $\frac{49}{100}$
B. $\frac{13}{20}$; $\frac{17}{100}$
C. 1; $\frac{3}{50}$
D. $\frac{2}{25}$; $\frac{4}{5}$
E. $\frac{3}{10}$; $\frac{7}{25}$
F. $\frac{1}{4}$; $\frac{93}{100}$
G. $\frac{1}{20}$; $\frac{1}{25}$
H. $\frac{7}{100}$; $\frac{2}{5}$
I. $\frac{9}{10}$; $\frac{3}{100}$
J. $\frac{3}{5}$; $\frac{17}{20}$
K. $\frac{1}{100}$; $\frac{23}{50}$

Page 47
A. 1.5; $1\frac{1}{2}$
B. 1.2; $1\frac{1}{5}$
C. 0.0003; $\frac{3}{10,000}$
D. 0.005; $\frac{1}{200}$
E. 0.069; $\frac{69}{1,000}$
F. 0.875; $\frac{7}{8}$
G. 6.0; 6
H. 0.025; $\frac{1}{40}$
I. 0.009; $\frac{9}{1,000}$
J. 1.23; $1\frac{23}{100}$
K. 2.27; $2\frac{27}{100}$
L. 2.5; $2\frac{1}{2}$
M. 0.024; $\frac{3}{125}$
N. 3.126; $3\frac{63}{500}$
O. 0.0025; $\frac{1}{400}$
P. 0.375; $\frac{3}{8}$
Q. 0.125; $\frac{1}{8}$
R. 0.0045; $\frac{9}{2,000}$
S. 4.107; $4\frac{107}{1,000}$
T. 0.123; $\frac{123}{1,000}$

Page 48
A. 54; 15
B. 1.2; 127.5; 61.74
C. 52; 9; 3.2
D. 75; 15; 255
E. 112; 36; 50
F. 17.5; 195; 54
G. 31; 32; 33.8

Page 49
A. 40%
B. 72%; 68%
C. 60%; 50%
D. 20%; 30%
E. 20%; 12.5%

Page 50
A. 500
B. 500; 32
C. 300; 160
D. 250; 60
E. 12; 500

Page 51
A. $72
B. $240; $160; $140
C. $731.50; $360; $675
D. $140; $357; $88

Page 52
A. Fiction—25,000
   Reference—30,000
   Nonfiction—20,000
   Books on Tape—5,000
   Children's—15,000
   Maps—5,000
B. Fiction—5,125
   Reference—6,150
   Nonfiction—4,100
   Books on Tape—1,025
   Children's—3,075
   Maps—1,025
C. 15,000 books

© Frank Schaffer Publications, Inc.   FS-11039 Pre-Algebra Activities

Georgina's Famous Chili

Here are the ingredients Georgina uses in her chili.

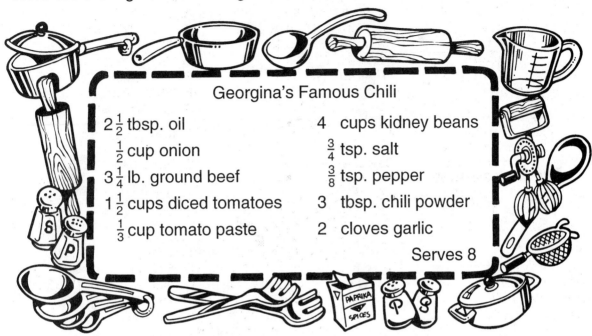

Georgina's Famous Chili

$2\frac{1}{2}$ tbsp. oil

$\frac{1}{2}$ cup onion

$3\frac{1}{4}$ lb. ground beef

$1\frac{1}{2}$ cups diced tomatoes

$\frac{1}{3}$ cup tomato paste

4 cups kidney beans

$\frac{3}{4}$ tsp. salt

$\frac{3}{8}$ tsp. pepper

3 tbsp. chili powder

2 cloves garlic

Serves 8

Revise the amount of each ingredient to serve the number of people shown.

Ingredient	16 servings	4 servings	20 servings	6 servings
oil	5 tbsp.	$1\frac{1}{4}$ tbsp.	$6\frac{1}{4}$ tbsp.	$1\frac{7}{8}$ tbsp.
onion				
ground beef				
tomatoes				
tomato paste				
kidney beans				
salt				
pepper				
chili powder				
garlic				

How Many Vowels?

Complete the frequency distribution table by tallying the vowels in the following paragraph. (The cumulative frequency is the sum of the frequency and all the frequencies above it on the table.)

> The alphabet consists of 26 letters. Five of them are vowels. Some vowels are used more often than others. Which do you think is used most in this paragraph?

Vowels Used in Everyday Writing

Vowel	Tally	Frequency	Cumulative Frequency

Use the frequency table to answer the questions.

A. How many vowels were used in the paragraph?

_____

B. How many more times was **o** used than **u**?

_____

C. How many times was either **a** or **e** used in the paragraph?

_____

D. Was **e** used more often or less often than the other vowels combined?

_____

Line Up

A line plot shows how numbers are distributed. Make a dot on the line plot to record each height listed in the box. Then cross off the number in the box.

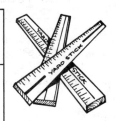

Heights of Students in Ms. Gagnon's Class (inches)						
56	59	52	57	58	57	63
59	59	63	64	59	61	57
55	66	60	66	57	64	58
60	57	67	57	61	58	59

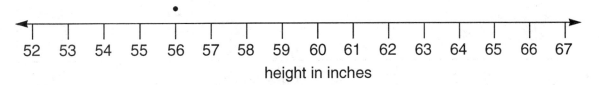

52 53 54 55 56 57 58 59 60 61 62 63 64 65 66 67

height in inches

Use the line plot to answer the questions.

A. Which height is most common to this class?

_____

B. What is the difference (in inches) between the shortest and the tallest student in the class?

_____

C. How many students are 63 inches tall or taller?

_____

D. How many students are 56 inches tall or shorter?

_____

E. Which heights on the line are not represented by the students in Ms. Gagnon's class?

_____

F. How many students are between 54 and 62 inches tall?

_____

Stem-and-Leaf Plots

Make a stem-and-leaf plot to organize the test scores listed in the box. In the *stem* column, write the tens digits of the scores in order from least to greatest. In the *leaves* column, write the digits that go with the tens digits in order from least to greatest. Cross off each number as you record it.

Test Scores for Ms. Woo's Math Class			
56	59	83	68
63	67	95	78
74	95	74	92
82	87	88	95
65	88	86	89
76	79	80	76
82	90	90	92

Stem	Leaves
5	6, 9

Use your stem-and-leaf plot to answer the questions.

A. What was the lowest score?

_____

B. What was the highest score?

_____

C. How many students scored 90 or above?

_____

D. How many students scored below 70?

_____

E. How many students scored between 70 and 89?

_____

F. What single score was the most common in Ms. Woo's class?

_____

Picture This

Make a pictograph for the data shown in the table below. Write a title on the line above the graph and make a symbol key. List the sports along the left side of the graph and use symbols to indicate the number of people who participate in each.

Mountain Climbing	60 people
Walking	120 people
Running	75 people
Swimming	30 people
Bicycling	45 people
Aerobics	15 people

_____

key

Use your pictograph to answer the questions.

A. Why did you choose your title?

_____

B. What does each symbol represent?

_____

Bars for Cars

Make a double bar graph for the data shown at the right. List the autos along the left side of the graph. For each car, show the number sold in March with one color and the number sold in April with another color. Write a title on the line above the graph and fill in the color key.

	March	April
Compact	2,000	2,300
2-Door Sports	1,200	1,800
4-Door Sedan	1,100	950
Station Wagon	900	850
Van	1,750	2,300

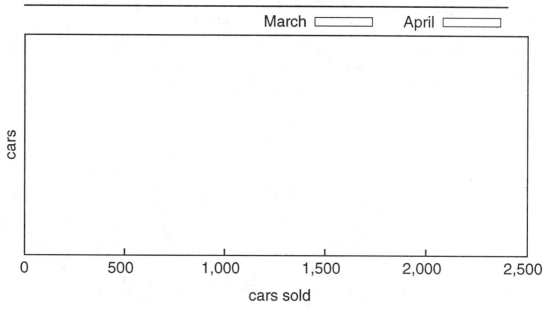

March ☐   April ☐

cars

0   500   1,000   1,500   2,000   2,500

cars sold

Use the information given to answer the questions.

A. Which car sales did not increase between March and April?

_____

B. Which car style had the largest increase in sales?

_____

C. How many more compact cars were sold in April than in March?

_____

D. Which two car styles had the same sales in April?

_____

Video Rental Records

Day of Week	Number of Videos
Mon.	60
Tues.	48
Wed.	60
Thurs.	72
Fri.	108
Sat.	120
Sun.	96

Make a line graph for the data shown on the chart at the right. Write a title on the line above the graph. Put labels along the horizontal and vertical axes. Make a dot to show the number of videos rented each day. Connect the dots with lines.

Use your line graph to answer the questions.

A. On which day were video rentals highest? Lowest?

B. On which two days were video rentals the same?

Heavyweight Histogram

Study the histogram below. Then answer the questions.

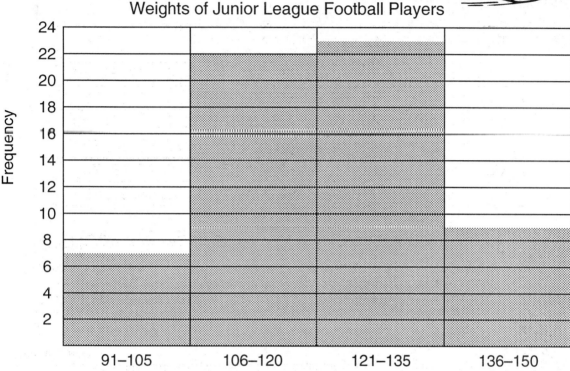

A. What does the width of each bar on the histogram represent?

_____

B. What does the height of each bar on the histogram represent?

_____

C. How many players weigh more than 135 pounds? _____

D. What is the weight range with the greatest frequency? _____

E. How many players weigh less than 106 pounds? _____

Measures of Central Tendency

Eleven students from each math class competed in a math competition. Their scores are shown below.

Teacher	Scores
Ms. Rowe	79, 83, 96, 75, 100, 80, 91, 87, 72, 86, 79
Mrs. Midgely	86, 89, 93, 86, 95, 82, 77, 86, 95, 98, 86
Mr. Maynard	68, 95, 72, 100, 82, 85, 72, 73, 68, 72, 80
Mr. Arnaiz	80, 75, 78, 80, 92, 66, 70, 78, 68, 90, 78
Ms. Silver	73, 68, 75, 82, 69, 85, 75, 78, 75, 88, 78
Ms. Choi	94, 90, 85, 87, 72, 79, 86, 95, 94, 98, 89

range
the difference between the least and greatest numbers

mean
the average

median
the middle number in a set of data

mode
the number that occurs most frequently in a set of data

Find the range, the mean to the nearest tenth, the median, and the mode for each class. Write them on the chart below.

Teacher	Range	Mean	Median	Mode
Ms. Rowe				
Mrs. Midgely				
Mr. Maynard				
Mr. Arnaiz				
Ms. Silver				
Ms. Choi				

Box-and-Whisker Graphs

A box-and-whisker graph organizes data and helps you interpret it. Study the box-and-whisker graph shown below. The **median** is the middle number in the ordered data. The **first quartile** is the median of the lower half of the data. The **third quartile** is the median of the upper half of the data.

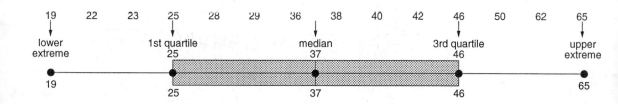

Answer the following questions about the box-and-whisker graph below.

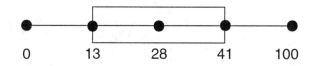

A. What is the lower extreme? _____

B. What is the first quartile? _____

C. What is the median? _____

D. What is the third quartile? _____

E. What is the upper extreme? _____

Simplest Ratios

Write each ratio as a fraction in its simplest form.

A.   15 to 5 = $\dfrac{15}{5} = \dfrac{3}{1}$ _____

B.   24 : 16 = _____ $\dfrac{8}{14}$ = _____

C. $\dfrac{26}{10}$ = _____   9 to 27 = _____

D.   10 : 34 = _____   16 to 36 = _____

E. $\dfrac{36}{24}$ = _____   7 to 35 = _____

F.   8 : 64 = _____   28 : 7 = _____

G.   64 to 36 = _____   48 : 144 = _____

H.   24 : 00 – _____ $\dfrac{18}{36}$ = _____

I.   15 to 18 = _____ $\dfrac{20}{45}$ = _____

J. $\dfrac{10}{14}$ = _____   25 to 45 = _____

K.   40 to 60 = _____   15 to 100 = _____

Rate Per Unit

A **rate** is a ratio that compares quantities of different units. A **unit rate** is a ratio that has 1 as the second term. Write the unit rate for each rate listed below.

A. 48 people in 6 vans

8 in 1

_____

150 kilometers in 3 hours

_____

B. 30 pounds in 6 weeks

_____

1,250 words in 5 minutes

_____

C. 90 people in 15 cars

_____

100 cards in 4 packages

_____

D. 48 months in 4 years

_____

144 markers in 6 boxes

_____

E. 550 miles in 10 hours

_____

720 minutes in 4 trips

_____

F. 258 kilometers in 3 hours

_____

300 people in 6 buses

_____

G. 160 pages in 4 hours

_____

266 rides in 7 weeks

_____

Is It a Proportion?

A **proportion** is an equation that has two equivalent ratios. Look at each pair of ratios below. Circle **Y** (yes) if they form a proportion. Circle **N** (no) if they do not.

A. $\frac{7}{3}$ and $\frac{14}{6}$ (Y) N $\frac{2}{3}$ and $\frac{10}{12}$ Y N $\frac{8}{4}$ and $\frac{6}{2}$ Y N

B. $\frac{2}{3}$ and $\frac{8}{12}$ Y N $\frac{2}{5}$ and $\frac{3}{10}$ Y N $\frac{2}{7}$ and $\frac{4}{14}$ Y N

C. $\frac{8}{12}$ and $\frac{12}{15}$ Y N $\frac{8}{3}$ and $\frac{16}{6}$ Y N $\frac{28}{21}$ and $\frac{8}{6}$ Y N

D. $\frac{2}{3}$ and $\frac{4}{9}$ Y N $\frac{3}{5}$ and $\frac{9}{15}$ Y N $\frac{4}{7}$ and $\frac{8}{14}$ Y N

E. $\frac{4}{10}$ and $\frac{6}{15}$ Y N $\frac{7}{12}$ and $\frac{3}{4}$ Y N $\frac{12}{54}$ and $\frac{2}{9}$ Y N

F. $\frac{5}{7}$ and $\frac{35}{49}$ Y N $\frac{4}{14}$ and $\frac{6}{21}$ Y N $\frac{12}{25}$ and $\frac{60}{125}$ Y N

G. $\frac{7}{9}$ and $\frac{63}{88}$ Y N $\frac{9}{13}$ and $\frac{45}{72}$ Y N $\frac{6}{15}$ and $\frac{45}{150}$ Y N

H. $\frac{10}{5}$ and $\frac{15}{10}$ Y N $\frac{4}{9}$ and $\frac{16}{36}$ Y N $\frac{8}{2}$ and $\frac{40}{10}$ Y N

I. $\frac{1}{7}$ and $\frac{10}{70}$ Y N $\frac{43}{85}$ and $\frac{86}{160}$ Y N $\frac{2}{9}$ and $\frac{27}{4}$ Y N

J. $\frac{15}{9}$ and $\frac{75}{45}$ Y N $\frac{63}{7}$ and $\frac{9}{1}$ Y N

Solving Proportions

You can cross multiply to find the missing number in a proportion. Use mental math or a calculator to find the missing numbers in the proportions listed below.

```
┌─────────────────────────────────────────────────┐
│        Mental Math          Calculator Math       │
│         3   9                  3   9               │
│         ─ = ──                 ─ = ──              │
│         n   21                 n   21              │
│   3 x 3 = 9 so n x 3 = 21    Cross multiply.       │
│       n must be 7            3 x 21 = 9 x n        │
│                               63 = 9 x n           │
│                              n must be 7           │
└─────────────────────────────────────────────────┘
```

A. $\dfrac{3}{8} = \dfrac{12}{n}$ $\dfrac{5}{6} = \dfrac{n}{12}$

n = _____   n = _____

B. $\dfrac{n}{6} = \dfrac{33}{18}$ $\dfrac{16}{72} = \dfrac{n}{9}$ $\dfrac{n}{40} = \dfrac{6}{10}$ $\dfrac{n}{5} = \dfrac{16}{20}$

n = _____   n = _____   n = _____   n = _____

C. $\dfrac{8}{12} = \dfrac{6}{n}$ $\dfrac{3}{9} = \dfrac{n}{15}$ $\dfrac{15}{5} = \dfrac{12}{n}$ $\dfrac{1}{2} = \dfrac{n}{4.2}$

n = _____   n = _____   n = _____   n = _____

D. $\dfrac{15}{20} = \dfrac{n}{4}$ $\dfrac{1}{12} = \dfrac{1.5}{n}$ $\dfrac{4}{5} = \dfrac{36}{n}$ $\dfrac{8}{5} = \dfrac{6}{n}$

n = _____   n = _____   n = _____   n = _____

E. $\dfrac{2}{n} = \dfrac{5}{7.5}$ $\dfrac{14}{8} = \dfrac{n}{20}$ $\dfrac{n}{0.8} = \dfrac{7}{8}$ $\dfrac{10}{13} = \dfrac{30}{n}$

n = _____   n = _____   n = _____   n = _____

Unit Pricing

Find the unit prices. Round to the nearest cent if necessary.

A.   3 for $0.96   7 for $1.61

_____   _____

B.   9 for $0.54   4 for $1.76   5 for $1.55

_____   _____   _____

C.   5 for $19.95   6 for $1.41 $1\frac{1}{2}$ for $3.45

_____   _____   _____

D.   12 for $13.32   4 for $5.00   3 for $2.91

_____   _____   _____

E.   3 for $228.00   20 for $45.00   8 for $4.68

_____   _____   _____

F. $2\frac{1}{4}$ for $1.00   8 for $10.00   5 for $67.00

_____   _____   _____

G.   5 for $18.75   11 for $1.21   16 for $8.80

_____   _____   _____

H.   3 for $4.74   4 for $3.00   18 for $50.00

_____   _____   _____

Bargain Shopping

Find the unit price for the items in each pair. Round to the nearest cent if necessary. Circle the best value in each pair.

A.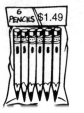

B.

_____   _____

C.

D.

_____   _____

E.

F.

_____   _____

G.

H.

_____   _____

42

Same Shape but Different Dimensions

Write the measurements of each pair of figures as a proportion to find the missing number.

A.

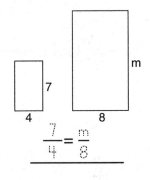

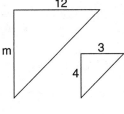

$$\frac{7}{4} = \frac{m}{8}$$
_____

$56 = 4m$
_____

$m = 14$
_____

_____

_____

_____

_____

_____

_____

B.

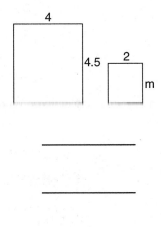

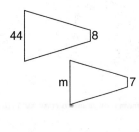

_____

_____

_____

_____

_____

_____

_____

_____

_____

Writing Percents

Write each decimal or fraction as a percent.

Percent means "out of 100."

A. $\frac{35}{100}$ = _____ $\frac{17}{100}$ = _____

B. 0.41 = _____   0.45 = _____

C. 0.23 = _____ $\frac{75}{100}$ = _____   0.72 = _____

D. $\frac{81}{100}$ = _____   0.01 = _____ $\frac{25}{100}$ = _____

E. $\frac{27}{100}$ = _____ $\frac{1}{2}$ = _____ $\frac{43}{100}$ = _____

F. 0.31 = _____   0.1 = _____ $\frac{4}{10}$ = _____

G. 0.05 = _____ $\frac{39}{100}$ = _____ $\frac{6}{10}$ = _____

H. $\frac{9}{100}$ = _____ $\frac{8}{10}$ = _____   0.08 = _____

I. 0.63 = _____   0.2 = _____ $\frac{45}{100}$ = _____

J. 0.71 = _____   0.86 = _____ $\frac{23}{100}$ = _____

K. $\frac{97}{100}$ = _____ $\frac{7}{100}$ = _____ $\frac{7}{10}$ = _____

Making Decimals From Percents

To change a percent to a decimal, move the decimal point two digits to the left.
Change each percent below to a decimal.

46% = 0.46

A. 95% = ___0.95___   82% = _____   43% = _____

B. 17% = _____   68% = _____   48% = _____

C. 71% = _____   4% = _____   73% = _____

D. 55% = _____   30% = _____   10% = _____

E.   7% = _____   15% = _____   9% = _____

F. 84% = _____   52% = _____   32% = _____

G. 94% = _____   2% = _____   11% = _____

H. 50% = _____   34% = _____   5% = _____

I. 19% – _____   100% = _____   26% = _____

J.   _____   20% = _____   1% = ___ 16% = ___

K. 12% = _____   21% = _____   51% = _____

L.   6% = _____   18% = _____   3% = _____

Making Fractions From Percents

Write each percent below as a fraction with a denominator of 100. Then write the fraction in its simplest form.

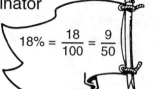

$$18\% = \frac{18}{100} = \frac{9}{50}$$

A.   49% = _____

B.   65% = _____   17% = _____

C.   100% = _____   6% = _____

D.   8% = _____   80% = _____

E.   30% = _____   28% = _____

F.   25% = _____   93% = _____

G.   5% = _____   4% = _____

H.   7% = _____   40% = _____

I.   90% = _____   3% = _____

J.   60% = _____   85% = _____

K.   1% = _____   46% = _____

Special Percents

Write each percent in decimal form
and as a fraction or mixed number.

Percent	Decimal	Fraction or Mixed Number	Percent	Decimal	Fraction or Mixed Number
A. 150%	1.5	$1\frac{1}{2}$	K. 227%		
B. 120%			L. 250%		
C. 0.03%			M. 2.4%		
D. 0.5 %			N. 312.6%		
E. 6.9%			O. 0.25%		
F. 87.5%			P. 37.5%		
G. 600%			Q. 12.5%		
H. 2.5%			R. 0.45%		
I. 0.9%			S. 410.7%		
J. 123%			T. 12.3%		

FS-11039 Pre-Algebra Activities

Percent of a Number

Find the percent of each number by using a calculator or by changing the percents to fractions or decimals and multiplying.

75% of 96 $\dfrac{3}{\cancel{4}} \times \dfrac{\cancel{96}^{24}}{1} = 72$	**A.** 50% of 108	30% of 50
B. 6% of 20	85% of 150	42% of 147
C. 80% of 65	30% of 30	8% of 40
D. 150% of 50	25% of 60	300% of 85
E. 28% of 400	75% of 48	25% of 200
F. 35% of 50	39% of 500	60% of 90
G. 25% of 124	$33\frac{1}{3}$% of 96	26% of 130

Missing Percents

Set up a proportion to find each missing percent. Circle the percent.

What percent of 20 is 3?

$$\frac{n}{100} = \frac{3}{20}$$

$$20n = 300$$

$$n = 15 \qquad \frac{15}{100} = \boxed{15\%}$$

A. What percent of 55 is 22?

B. What percent of 25 is 18?

What percent of 50 is 34?

C. What percent of 75 is 45?

What percent of 78 is 39?

D. 15 is what percent of 75?

18 is what percent of 60?

E. What percent of 40 is 8?

3 is what percent of 24?

Missing Numbers

Set up a proportion to find each missing number. Circle the number.

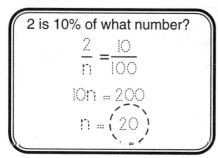

2 is 10% of what number?

$$\frac{2}{n} = \frac{10}{100}$$

$10n = 200$

$n = \boxed{20}$

A. 15% of what number is 75?

B. 20 is 4% of what number?

75% of what number is 24?

C. 60 is 20% of what number?

40 is 25% of what number?

D. 15 is 6% of what number?

25% of what number is 15?

E. 6 is 50% of what number?

270 is 54% of what number?

Simple Interest

Find the interest using the formula **Interest = principal • rate • time.**
You may use a calculator if you wish.

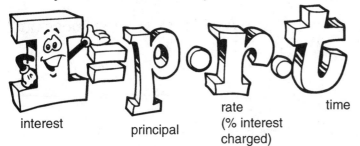

interest   principal   rate (% interest charged)   time

A.   p = $600
r = 12% per year
t = 1 year

I = _____

B.   p = $400
r = 12% per year
t = 5 years

I = _____

p = $800
r = 10% per year
t = 2 years

I = _____

p = $2,000
r = 14% per year
t = $\frac{1}{2}$ year

I = _____

C.   p = $950
r = 22% per year
t = $3\frac{1}{2}$ years

I = _____

p = $1,200
r = 12% per year
t = $2\frac{1}{2}$ years

I = _____

p = $1,250
r = 18% per year
t = 3 years

I = _____

D.   p = $400
r = 1% per month
t = 35 months

I = _____

p = $600
r = 17% per year
t = $3\frac{1}{2}$ years

I = _____

p = $800
r = 22% per year
t = $\frac{1}{2}$ year

I = _____

Statistics From a Circle

Use the percentages given on the graph to calculate the answers to the questions. Assume that each library has the distribution of books shown on the graph.

A. The Village Library has a total of 100,000 books. How many books does it have in each category?

Fiction _____

Reference _____

Nonfiction _____

Books on Tape _____

Children's _____

Maps _____

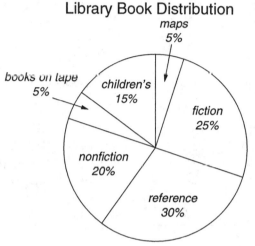

Library Book Distribution

maps 5%

books on tape 5%

children's 15%

fiction 25%

nonfiction 20%

reference 30%

B. The new North River Library has 20,500 books. How many books does it have in each category?

Fiction _____   Reference _____

Nonfiction _____   Books on Tape _____

Children's _____   Maps _____

C. If a library has 3,000 nonfiction books, how many books does it have in all?

_____